AL EAST

BALTIMORE

ORIOLES

ADMIT ONE

RICHARD RAMBECK

Published by Creative Education, Inc.

123 S. Broad Street, Mankato, Minnesota 56001

Art Director, Rita Marshall
Cover and title page design by Virginia Evans
Cover and title page illustration by Rob Day
Type set by FinalCopy Electronic Publishing
Book design by Rita Marshall

Photos by Allsport, Duomo, Focus on Sports,
Michael Ponzini, Bruce Schwartzman,
Sportschrome West, Sports Illustrated, UPI/Bettmann
and Wide World Photos

Library of Congress Cataloging-in-Publication Data

Rambeck, Richard.

  Baltimore Orioles / by Richard Rambeck.

  p.   cm.

  Summary: A team history of the Baltimore Orioles,
a team that migrated from St. Louis in 1952.

  ISBN 0-88682-451-6

  1. Baltimore Orioles (Baseball team)—History—
Juvenile literature. [1. Baltimore Orioles (Baseball
team)—History.   2. Baseball—History.]   I. Title.
GV875.B2R36 1991   91-2480
796.357'64'097526—dc20   CIP

THE EARLY YEARS

Much of the economic activity in the state of Maryland is centered on its largest city, Baltimore, which is one of the busiest ports in the United States. Located on beautiful Chesapeake Bay, Baltimore has been one of this country's largest cities since colonial days. In fact, in 1850 only New York City had more citizens than Baltimore.

The city is named after the man responsible for one of the earliest settlements in Maryland, Cecilius Calvert, who was known as Lord Baltimore. The British government granted land in the colonies to Calvert in 1632, and his brother led a group of two hundred settlers to an area near the St. Mary's River, a region that eventually became the bustling city of Baltimore.

Baltimore shortstop Mark Belanger.

Baltimore is known for trade, but the city also has played a big role in U.S. history. Francis Scott Key composed the *Star-Spangled Banner,* our national anthem, at Baltimore's Fort McHenry in 1814. Key wrote the famous song during a decisive battle in the War of 1812, when the British fleet attempted to capture the fort.

Part of Baltimore's rich history is a baseball team that, since it moved to the Maryland city in 1954, has had one of the finest records in baseball. The team, nicknamed the Orioles after Maryland's state bird, has given the Baltimore fans a lot to cheer about during the last four decades, including three World Series championships and six American League pennants.

The Baltimore franchise actually began life in St. Louis. Known as the Browns, the St. Louis club was one of the least successful teams in the American League. It joined the league in 1902, but didn't win a pennant until 1944, when, led by Vern Stephens, who topped the American League in runs batted in with 109, the team posted an 89–65 record. In the World Series, the Browns faced their crosstown rivals, the St. Louis Cardinals. The Cards had claimed their third consecutive National League title, with an incredible 105–49 record, but the Browns weren't intimidated. St. Louis's "other" team won two of the first three games of the series. The Cardinals, however, rallied to take the last three outings, winning the World Series four games to two.

A year after playing in the World Series, the Browns fell to last place. By 1951, when Bill Veeck bought the team, the Browns were among the worst clubs in the majors. They were also losers at the box office: in 1952, St. Louis lost a half-million dollars. Veeck decided the

6   *Oriole great, Boog Powell.*

team's future was not in St. Louis; he looked around and found a group in Baltimore interested in buying the Browns. The group, led by Baltimore attorney Clarence W. Miles, purchased the club for $2,475,000. The Browns moved to Maryland in 1954 and changed their name to the Orioles.

The Baltimore fans, who had long supported minor-league teams, immediately fell in love with their new club. More than one million fans saw the Orioles play in 1954, when they finished seventh in the eight-team American League. The fan support enabled the club to make a profit of nearly one million dollars. But the team still wasn't successful. Clearly, some of that money had to be used to develop young talent. General Manager Lindsay Deal already had his eye on a prospect, a third baseman named Brooks Robinson.

In their second season in Baltimore, new manager Paul Richards led the Orioles to a 57–97 mark.

BROOKS ROBINSON FIELDS SMOOTHLY

On February 13, 1955, Deal wrote a letter to a former teammate, Paul Richards, who would soon replace Deal as general manager. "Dear Paul, I am writing you in regard to a kid named Brooks Robinson," Deal wrote. "I think he measures up to having a chance in major-league baseball. I think he is a natural third baseman, although he has been playing both second and third. He will be 18 years old May 18 and graduates from Little Rock Senior High School on May 27. . . . This boy is the best prospect I've seen since Billy Goodman came to Atlanta to play when I was playing there."

Deal proved to have a good eye for talent. The Orioles

signed Robinson, and seven months after Deal had written Richards, Robinson became the first prospect to make the team since it had left St. Louis. Robinson brought two outstanding attributes to the Orioles: his great fielding and his great attitude. His two basic beliefs were "All's well that ends well" and "Most things do end well."

In 1959 Robinson's baseball career nearly came to an abrupt end. Chasing a foul ball into a dugout, Robinson caught his arm on a steel hook, cutting several nerves and tendons. While doctors took twenty-two stitches in his arm, he joked with the nurses, even though he knew he might never bend his elbow again. Six weeks later Robinson had fought his way back into the lineup.

1 9 6 1

Big James Gentile slammed 46 homers, including 5 grand slams for the Orioles.

Robinson also had to fight through occasional hitting slumps early in his career. One season team officials had decided to send Robinson down to the minor leagues to regain his batting stroke, but a group of Baltimore pitchers went to General Manager Paul Richards and begged him to keep Robinson on the team. "They didn't care if he never got a hit," Richards said. The pitchers wanted him in the game for his fielding. Eventually, Robinson's hitting would improve with experience. In 1964 he led the American League in runs batted in with 118. Despite Robinson's heroics, though, the Orioles were not pennant contenders—not, that is, until 1966.

FRANK ROBINSON PROVES TO BE A TRIPLE THREAT

The Orioles made a bold trade before the 1966 season began, sending Milt Pappas, Dick Simpson, and Jack Baldschun to the Cincinnati Reds for right

A Brooks Robinson-like effort.

A Baltimore trademark—aggressive baserunning.   11

In his first season in Baltimore Frank Robinson (right) won the AL Triple Crown and was league MVP.

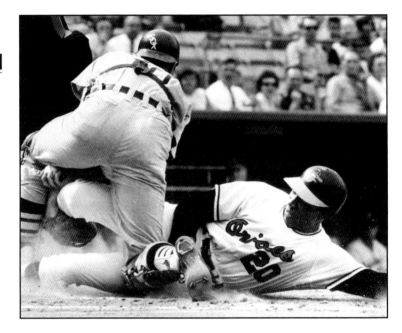

fielder Frank Robinson. Robinson had been a star for years in the National League. Many experts, however, believed Robinson's best days were behind him. They couldn't have been more mistaken. Baltimore manager Hank Bauer put the two Robinsons back-to-back in the batting order, and it paid off immediately.

In Baltimore's first four games of 1966, each Robinson had three home runs; in addition Brooks had eight RBI, Frank six. In fact, in their first thirty-two games that season, the Robinsons accounted for twenty-four game-winning runs, go-ahead runs, or runs that brought the Orioles within one of a tie. Frank Robinson dazzled the Oriole fans by clouting a 540-foot home run that sailed over the bleacher wall in Baltimore's Memorial Stadium; he was the first player ever to do that. "He really creamed it," Brooks Robinson said. "He's a tremendous guy to be playing with and to hit behind. He gets on base so often, and he can steal and set up a run for us."

Frank Robinson was a bold hitter who crowded the plate and often led the major leagues in number of times hit by pitches. "Nobody has ever had more guts at the plate than Frank," said Earl Weaver, who would become the Orioles manager in 1968. "He actually curled his upper body and head over the plate and dared pitchers to hit him."

1 9 6 6

Led by Dave McNally, the Orioles held LA to 33 consecutive scoreless innings in the World Series.

The player the Cincinnati Reds thought was washed up had a remarkable year in 1966. He wound up leading the American League in homers (forty-nine), runs batted in (122), and batting average (.316), making him the first American Leaguer since Mickey Mantle in 1956 to claim the Triple Crown. Named the American League's Most Valuable Player, he led the Orioles to their first-ever AL pennant. In the World Series against the Los Angeles Dodgers, both Robinsons had home runs as the Orioles shocked the favored Dodgers with a four-games-to-none sweep. As good as the Robinsons were in the series, though, the Baltimore pitching was even better. Dave McNally, Wally Bunker, and a twenty-year-old phenom named Jim Palmer shut down Los Angeles. Actually, they shut the Dodgers out—L.A. didn't score a run in the last three games of the series.

Unfortunately, the Orioles were unable to maintain their championship ways. Hank Bauer was fired as manager in the middle of the 1968 season and replaced by Earl Weaver, who had coached Baltimore's top minor-league team. Weaver inherited a team of players who disliked each other almost as much as they disliked Bauer. When he took over, Weaver told the players that

The towering Boog Powell terrorized opposing pitchers by slamming 37 homers and driving in 121 runs.

his door was always open and that they should feel free to bring their complaints to him. The players heard Weaver's speech and then left. Weaver walked back to his office; minutes later Frank Robinson stopped by. "The only player who walked into my office after the meeting was Frank Robinson," Weaver said. "The best player in all of baseball said, 'If there's anything I can do to help, let me know.' I appreciated that."

It also gave Weaver the opportunity to assume command. He had Robinson, a player all of the Orioles looked up to and listened to, behind him. Suddenly, the Orioles started to play much better, going 48–34 in the games Weaver managed at the end of the 1968 season. The ingredients were in place for another pennant run in 1969.

Before the season, the Orioles, who already had two fine starting pitchers in Dave McNally and Jim Palmer, added another standout starter in a trade with the Houston Astros, Mike Cuellar. In 1969 Cuellar would be co-winner (with Detroit pitcher Denny McLain) of the Cy Young Award. Led by Cuellar, the Orioles dominated the race in the American League East Division. (The league was divided into two divisions before the 1969 season.) Baltimore won 109 games, the most victories by a major-league team in eight years. The Orioles had great hitting from Frank Robinson, Boog Powell, and outfielders Paul Blair and Don Buford. The team also had great fielders: Brooks Robinson, shortstop Mark Belanger, second baseman Dave Johnson, and center fielder Blair were all outstanding.

Led by these stars, Baltimore swept AL West winner Minnesota in the American League Championship Series.

The 1969 Orioles were above all competition.

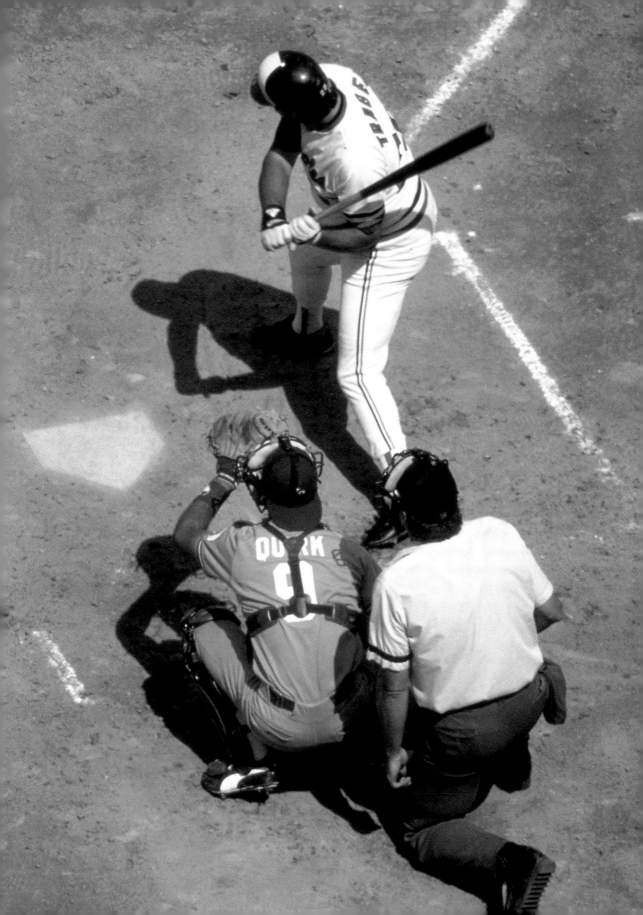

In the World Series, however, the Orioles ran into destiny—and the amazing New York Mets, who, not long before, had been one of the worst teams in baseball. After Cuellar pitched Baltimore to a 4–1 victory in game one, the Mets rallied behind pitchers Tom Seaver and Jerry Koosman to take the series four games to one.

In 1970 the Orioles again romped to the AL East title, this time winning 108 games. The Orioles then beat Minnesota in the league championship series to earn the right to play "The Big Red Machine" of Cincinnati in the World Series. Many experts picked the Reds, but the Orioles, and Brooks Robinson in particular, were determined to win this series.

It didn't start well for Robinson and the Orioles, though. The first time a ball was hit to Brooks in the series, he made a bad throw that turned into a two-base

16

Baltimore ace Jim Palmer.   17

Current Oriole star Cal Ripken, Jr.

*For the second
consecutive year
Dave McNally (right)
won over 20 games
(21) for the Orioles.*

error. But an angry Robinson vowed not to let the mistake get to him, and it didn't. He proceeded to put on a fielding performance that is unmatched in World Series history. Several times he dove to snag sure base hits and turn them into outs. "I've seen all the greatest third baseman over the last fifty years—Home Run Baker, Pie Traynor, Eddie Mathews," said former New York Yankee manager Casey Stengel during the series. "I don't say he [Robinson] is any better than they were, but he compares with them. Don't hit it to that fellow."

Stengel might not have been sure that Robinson was the best third baseman ever, but Pie Traynor apparently thought he was. "I once thought of giving him some tips," Traynor said, "but dropped the idea. He's just the best there is." Led by Robinson, who was named Most

20

Valuable Player, the Orioles won the series four games to one.

A year later, in 1971, the Orioles won another American League East title and then defeated the Oakland Athletics to earn a spot in their third straight World Series. Among American League teams, only the New York Yankees, Philadelphia Athletics (who eventually became the Oakland Athletics), and Detroit Tigers had played in three consecutive World Series. The Orioles, however, did not win the 1971 series. After triumphing in the first two games against the Pittsburgh Pirates, Baltimore then dropped three in a row and eventually lost four games to three.

Baltimore ace Jim Palmer completed an Oriole team record 25 games during the season.

Despite the disappointment in the World Series, the Orioles remained one of the top teams in the American League. They won the AL East in 1973 and 1974, but lost both years to the eventual world-champion Oakland A's in the league championship series. By 1977, however, the Oriole stars had gotten old and, in some cases, had retired. Brooks Robinson was no longer around, and Frank Robinson had left to take a job as the manager of the Cleveland Indians, becoming the first black manager in major-league history.

Earl Weaver wondered how he would replace Frank Robinson. "He had great, great baseball instincts and tremendous physical attributes that allowed him to do everything right on a ball field," Weaver said. "It's sad to say, but Baltimore will never have another Frank Robinson." That may be true, but when Robinson left the Orioles, another leader emerged. This time it was a pitcher. His name: Jim Palmer.

The dangerous Eddie Murray.

PALMER MAKES A PITCH AT LEADERSHIP

Jim Palmer was one of the most dominant, if not *the* most dominant, major-league pitcher during the 1970s. His devastating high fastball, pinpoint control, and keen understanding of how to pitch made him a star of Hall-of-Fame quality. In fact, Palmer, who won three Cy Young Awards as the American League's top pitcher in 1973, 1975, and 1976, was elected to the Hall of Fame in 1990. "Palmer is a great pitcher, certainly one of the all-time greats," said Earl Weaver. "I can't count all the big games he has won for us. . . . He has risen to the occasion as much as any pitcher in baseball."

Ken Singleton was named the Orioles' MVP as he led the club to the AL East division title.

It was strange to hear Weaver praise Palmer, because the two usually were fighting, often through the newspapers and on television. Palmer, who suffered a lot of nagging injuries, would say he was unable to pitch, and Weaver would say the whole thing was in Palmer's head. Palmer may have fought with Weaver, but the Orioles' star pitcher was a role model for the younger players. "He is like having another pitching coach around," said Baltimore pitching coach Ray Miller. "When the other players see a guy like Palmer working hard and taking care of himself, it does more good than anything you can tell them."

Despite Palmer's leadership, the Orioles, who won five AL East titles in six years from 1969 to 1974, went without a division championship for the next five seasons. But the team was building a stable of new stars, including young pitchers Mike Flanagan and Scott McGregor, and first baseman Eddie Murray, who in 1977 was named Rookie of the Year in the American League. In 1979

24   *Left to right: Mike Flanagan, Mike Boddicker, Earl Weaver, Scott McGregor.*

Flanagan, who won the American League's Cy Young Award, and Palmer pitched the Orioles to an AL East Division title. Baltimore then beat the California Angels in the league championship series. For the first time in eight years, the Orioles had made it to the World Series. They had the same opponent, the Pittsburgh Pirates, as they had had eight years before. Unfortunately for the Orioles, the result was also the same: The Pirates beat Baltimore four games to three for the series title.

Righthander Steve Stone recorded twenty-five victories and earned the AL's Cy Young Award.

The 1979 American League pennant was to be the last the Orioles won under Earl Weaver, whose frustrations increased when Baltimore finished second in the division from 1980 through 1982. In 1982 the Milwaukee Brewers defeated the Orioles on the final day of the regular season to claim the AL East title. Weaver then announced his retirement. When the 1983 season began, the Orioles had a new manager for the first time in fifteen years: Joe Altobelli. They also had a new star: shortstop Cal Ripken, Jr.

RIPKEN IS A CHIP OFF THE OLD BLOCK

Cal Ripken, Jr., played his first season for the Orioles in 1982, but he had been around the club all of his life. Has father, Cal Ripken, Sr., had been a coach in the Baltimore system since before his son was born. Growing up, the younger Cal would often ride with his father to Oriole practices. "When dad first asked if I wanted to go to the ballpark with him, I went because I could be with him alone on the drive there and back," Ripken said. "Eventually I began to enjoy baseball." He also began to learn baseball. "I'd go ask someone, say [Baltimore third

After fourteen years as Baltimore manager Earl Weaver retired— only to return three years later.

baseman] Doug DeCinces, about how to do a certain thing. Then when he told me, I'd go ask my dad if what he told me was right. My dad was always the final authority, and if he told me the guy gave me correct information, I knew I could go back to him."

When Cal Ripken, Jr. joined the Orioles, it became impossible to move him out of the starting lineup. In fact, Ripken never missed an inning, let alone a game, during his first few years in the major leagues. His consecutive-game streak eventually would become the second longest in major-league history, behind only Lou Gehrig's streak of 2,130.

Ripken, who was named the American League Rookie of the Year in 1982, had an even better year in 1983, winning the Most Valuable Player Award. During the season he amassed 221 hits, scored 121 runs, and hit forty-seven doubles. Ripken, Eddie Murray, and designated hitter Ken Singleton powered the Oriole offense, and rookie pitcher Mike Boddicker filled in for the injured Jim Palmer and threw five shutouts.

Baltimore rolled to the AL East title and then defeated Chicago for the American League pennant. In the World Series, the Orioles lost the first game to the Philadelphia Phillies and then won four straight to claim their first World Series title since 1970.

The Orioles had reached the top again, but they would soon fall to the bottom. Altobelli was fired in 1985 and replaced by Earl Weaver, who quit after the 1987 season. Cal Ripken, Sr., started the 1988 season as manager, but he was replaced after the Orioles lost their first six games. Former star Frank Robinson was brought in as manager, but even he couldn't prevent the Orioles from posting

Relief pitcher Gregg Olson (left), set an Oriole record with 37 saves during the season.

the worst record in major-league baseball. Despite their awful record, though, the Orioles were making strides toward success. Robinson benched many older players and started giving more time to the younger talent. This would pay off in 1989.

The Orioles suddenly changed from awful to nearly awesome in 1989. Youngsters Jeff Ballard and Bob Milacki were solid starting pitchers, and rookie Gregg Olson posted twenty-seven saves and was named Rookie of the Year in the American League. Outfielder Joe Orsulak, third baseman Craig Worthington, and first baseman Randy Milligan teamed with Cal Ripken, Jr., to key the Baltimore offense. And veteran catcher Mickey Tettleton shocked everyone by hitting twenty-six home runs, easily a career high.

Oriole ace Ben McDonald.

Hard throwing Bob Milacki.

Led by the powerful Ben McDonald the Baltimore pitching staff became one of baseball's best.

The Orioles, who won only fifty four games in 1988, posted an 87–75 record in 1989, finishing a close second in the AL East to the Toronto Blue Jays. Baltimore actually led the division for most of the season before being overtaken by Toronto in September. In 1990, though, the team fell behind Boston and Toronto early in the season and never caught up. Both Ballard and Milacki had sub-par years, as did Craig Worthington.

The season's biggest highlights were the ninety-five-game errorless streak by Cal Ripken, Jr., a major-league record for shortstops, and the emergence of young power pitcher Ben McDonald. McDonald was called up from the minor leagues in mid-season and proceeded to win his first five starts. Although he lost his next three decisions, McDonald showed he has the potential to be one of the top pitchers in baseball for the next fifteen years.

McDonald's ability caused experts to compare him to such Oriole greats as Jim Palmer, Mike Cuellar, Mike Flanagan, and Dave McNally. Those were some of the players who led the Orioles to the top of the baseball world in the late 1960s and throughout the 1970s. It's that type of team that Oriole management believes can be built around the talents of McDonald, Cal Ripken, Jr., Gregg Olson, and several young players nearing stardom.